The Gateways
SHABBAT
Family Companion

By Rebecca Redner

Editorial Committee
Jenna Andelman
Jayne Beker
Rabbi Martin S. Cohen
Rachel Fadlon
Rabbi Ilana Garber
Dana Keil
Arlene Remz
Donald Wertlieb

Project Editor: Terry Kaye
Design: Studio Rinat Gilboa
Illustration: Rebecca Redner
Photography: Jordyn Rozensky

Copyright © 2016 Gateways: Access to Jewish Education
Published by Behrman House, Inc., Springfield, New Jersey | www.behrmanhouse.com
ISBN: 978-0-87441-996-2 | Manufactured in the United States of America

Dedication

Dedicated to Anita Redner z"l,
beloved wife, mother, sister, teacher, nurse, mentor, and friend.

We remember Anita for her outstanding contributions, devotion, and deep love for the many communities where she lived and worked. Anita made a difference in the lives of countless children and adults and will always have a place in our hearts.

Acknowledgments

Gateways deeply appreciates the generous support of:
Sisterhood Temple Emanuel, Newton, Massachusetts
and of
Friends of Hadassah's Landy Kaplan Nurses Council
Friends of the Redner Family
Gateways Staff
Simmons College "Sisters"
Solomon Schechter Day School of Greater Boston

We are grateful to the models pictured in this book, and especially to the Chafetz family for opening their home for the photo shoot. We extend our gratitude to all of the colleagues, friends, and family members who provided us with editorial guidance and emotional support. We would like to acknowledge all of the students of the Gateways Jewish Education Programs, past and present, whose enthusiasm for Jewish learning inspired this project. Thank you to my mother, Anita Redner, who taught me to appreciate the joys of Shabbat, and whose example shaped my identity as an educator.

Rebecca Redner
Gateways: Access to Jewish Education

Contents

Creation 4

What is Shabbat? 5

Setting the Shabbat Table.................... 6

Tzedakah 7

Lighting the Shabbat Candles 8

Blessing the Children 10

Shalom Aleichem 12

Shabbat Shalom 14

Blessing over the Wine 15

Washing Hands 16

Sending Messages without Talking 17

Blessing over the Bread 18

Shabbat Meal Conversation.................. 20

Blessing after Our Meal 21

What We Do on the Day of Shabbat 22

Havdalah 23

Talking to Children about God 24

Creation

In the beginning, there was nothing but God.

On day 1 God said, "Let there be light," and golden light appeared.

On day 2 God made the salty seas and the clear blue sky.

On day 3 God made the ground where soft grass, tall trees, and sweet-smelling flowers began to grow.

On day 4 God made the bright sun and the silvery moon, and filled the night sky with shiny stars.

On day 5 God made birds that soar through the air and fish that swim in the water.

On day 6 God made all kinds of animals and the first people: a man and a woman.

On day 7 God was finished creating the world. On day 7 God rested. We call this day of rest Shabbat.

What is Shabbat?

Do you sometimes feel tired or stressed at the end of a long week? That you haven't spent enough time with your family and friends or doing the things that you like? That's why we look forward to Shabbat — the day to stop working, restore our energy, and be with people we care about.

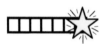

The Torah tells us that, long ago, God created our world in just six days. After finishing the work of Creation, God paused and rested for one day. We call that day Shabbat.

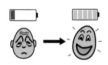

The Torah teaches that Shabbat is not only God's day of rest, but our day of rest too. Shabbat is for everyone: young and old, rich and poor, weak and strong. It is a day when we are all free to pause, restore our energy after a week of work, and spend time with family and friends.

Shabbat is different from the other days of the week. It is holy, a day on which we choose to do things to help ourselves feel closer to God. When we quiet our bodies and our minds on Shabbat, we can notice the beauty of the world and feel closer to the people we care about.

Shabbat begins each Friday night. Just before the sun sets, Jewish people around the world prepare to welcome Shabbat into their homes.

Setting the Shabbat Table

Imagine that a queen was coming to your house for dinner. Would you use your everyday dishes or your very best dishes? Would you put something extra on the table to make it beautiful, like a vase of sweet-smelling flowers, a silver cup, or a fine white tablecloth?

On Shabbat we set the table as if we were setting it for a queen, and we put objects on the table that we don't use during the other days of the week. What will you put on your Shabbat table? How can a beautiful Shabbat table help you feel joyful?

candles

Kiddush cup

bottle of wine or grape juice

challah

challah cover

kippot

flowers

a pretty tablecloth

nice dishes and silverware

Tzedakah

Before Shabbat we pause to think about other people. We sit at a table set with our nice dishes and eat a big, delicious meal. But some people are not able to celebrate Shabbat in this way. How do you think it feels to be hungry on Shabbat?

All people should be able to enjoy Shabbat. The Torah tells us that it's important to help people who don't have the things they need to be happy and healthy such as warm clothes and healthy food.

So before Shabbat begins, we put money in a tzedakah box. We will give that money to people who need it. The money from the tzedakah box can help people buy things they need to be happy and healthy.

Giving tzedakah is one small thing we can do to help other people. Starting Shabbat this way can give us a good feeling inside and help make the world a better place.

Lighting the Shabbat Candles

We light candles to celebrate the beginning of Shabbat tonight. The light of the candles creates a golden glow and makes the house feel cozy and warm.

Light the candles.

Usually an adult strikes the match and lights the candles. You can still be a part of lighting the candles by touching that adult's arm or putting your hand on the adult's hand.

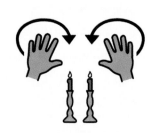

Carefully wave your hands over the candles three times.

Wave your hands as though you are pulling the light from the candles into your body. Feel the warmth of the candles fill your body.

Cover your eyes.

We wait to look at the candlelight until after we have said the blessing—that's why we cover our eyes while saying the blessing.

Say the blessing:

בָּרוּךְ אַתָּה יְיָ אֱלֹהֵינוּ מֶלֶךְ הָעוֹלָם,
אֲשֶׁר קִדְּשָׁנוּ בְּמִצְוֹתָיו וְצִוָּנוּ לְהַדְלִיק נֵר שֶׁל שַׁבָּת.

Baruch	atah	Adonai	Eloheinu	Melech	ha'olam

asher	kid'shanu	bemitzvotav	vetzivanu	lehadlik ner	shel Shabbat

Thank you God, Ruler of the world, who makes us holy with mitzvot and tells us to light candles on Shabbat.

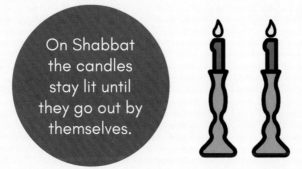

On Shabbat the candles stay lit until they go out by themselves.

Look at the eyes of the people around you. Can you see the light of the flames reflected in their eyes? They can see the light reflected in yours! Now we can all enjoy the light and warmth of the Shabbat candles together.

Blessing the Children

On Shabbat we pause and think about the ways we show our love for each other. Family members take care of each other and do nice things for each other. One way parents show their love is by asking God to be kind to their children and to help them have good lives. And everybody in the family can say loving things to one another.

Think about things the people in your family have done for you this past week. Maybe someone helped you, or did something fun with you, or made you feel good inside.

Take turns thanking each other and giving each other compliments.

When it's your turn, try to look at each person and thank them for the nice things they have done for you. You might also want to give that person a high five, a hug, or a kiss.

While the children stand still in one place, parents should put their hands on or close to the heads of the children and say the blessing for boys or girls:

Blessing for a boy:

יְשִׂמְךָ אֱלֹהִים כְּאֶפְרַיִם וְכִמְנַשֶּׁה.

Yesimcha Elohim ke

Ephraim ve chi Menashe

May God make you like Ephraim and Menashe.

Blessing for a girl:

יְשִׂמֵךְ אֱלֹהִים כְּשָׂרָה רִבְקָה רָחֵל וְלֵאָה.

Yesimech Elohim ke

Sarah Rivka Rachel ve Leah

May God make you like Sarah, Rebecca, Rachel, and Leah.

Now is a good time to say loving words to each other and give a hug or kiss.

Shalom Aleichem

 On Friday night Jewish families around the world pause what they're doing to get ready for Shabbat. They make their homes beautiful, clean, and cozy. They cook special foods and set the table with nice dishes.

 Rabbis long ago told a story about being ready for Shabbat. We still tell this Shabbat story today.

 The story says that two angels visit Jewish homes together each Friday night. The angels go to Jewish homes to see if candles are lit, the table is set, and everything is ready for Shabbat.

 If the home is all ready for Shabbat one angel smiles and says, "May next Shabbat be this bright and peaceful." Then the other angel replies, "Amen. May it be so."

 On Friday nights we remember this story and imagine what would happen if angels came to visit our homes. We imagine that we would greet the visiting angels by saying "shalom aleichem," Hebrew words of welcome meaning "peace to you."

שָׁלוֹם עֲלֵיכֶם מַלְאֲכֵי הַשָּׁרֵת מַלְאֲכֵי עֶלְיוֹן
מִמֶּלֶךְ מַלְכֵי הַמְּלָכִים הַקָּדוֹשׁ בָּרוּךְ הוּא,
בּוֹאֲכֶם לְשָׁלוֹם מַלְאֲכֵי הַשָּׁלוֹם מַלְאֲכֵי עֶלְיוֹן
מִמֶּלֶךְ מַלְכֵי הַמְּלָכִים הַקָּדוֹשׁ בָּרוּךְ הוּא.

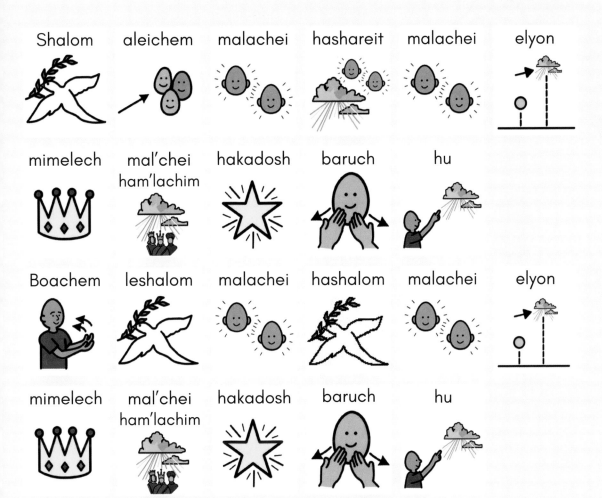

Welcome, helping angels, angels of God on high,
from the Ruler, the greatest Ruler, the Holy One, blessed be God.
Come in peace, angels of peace, angels of God on high,
from the Ruler, the greatest Ruler, the Holy One, blessed be God.

Shabbat Shalom

 "Shabbat shalom" means "peaceful Shabbat." When we say these words, we mean, "I hope you have a good and calm Shabbat."

 Let's pause to feel the peace of Shabbat. Take a slow breath in. As you breathe in, imagine that you are breathing in good and calm Shabbat feelings, and letting them fill your body.

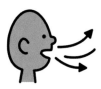 Then breathe out slowly. Imagine that you are blowing busy and stressful feelings out of your body. Feel them leave your body. And as you breathe out, let your body loosen and relax.

 Now that Shabbat has begun, it's time to wish each other a good and peaceful Shabbat! Try to look at somebody near you and say "Shabbat shalom."

Some family members and close friends hug or kiss each other when they say Shabbat shalom. It's okay if you don't feel comfortable hugging or kissing someone. You can shake that person's hand, give a fist bump, or smile.

Blessing over the Wine

We drink wine or grape juice to celebrate many Jewish holidays. The sweet taste of these drinks made from grapes reminds us of the joy of Shabbat, and helps us get ready to celebrate.

Pour wine or grape juice into your Kiddush cup.
How do you feel as you listen to the splash in your cup?

Hold your Kiddush cup.

Say the blessing:

בָּרוּךְ אַתָּה יְיָ אֱלֹהֵינוּ מֶלֶךְ הָעוֹלָם
בּוֹרֵא פְּרִי הַגָּפֶן.

Baruch	atah	Adonai	Eloheinu	Melech	ha'olam

borei   p'ri
         hagafen

Thank you God, Ruler of the world, who makes the fruit of the vine [grapes].

Drink your wine or grape juice. Sip it slowly and let its sweet taste fill your mouth.

If you don't want to drink any wine or grape juice, just put down the Kiddush cup.

Washing Hands

Before we eat we usually wash our hands with soap to clean off the dirt and germs. But before the Shabbat meal we also wash our hands for a different reason. Washing our hands with water and saying a blessing can help wash away the stressful feelings of the past week so we feel peaceful for Shabbat.

Pour water over both your hands.
Be sure to hold your hands over the sink or a bowl. How does the water feel as it gently flows over your hands?

Wipe your hands when you're done.

Say the blessing:

בָּרוּךְ אַתָּה יְיָ אֱלֹהֵינוּ מֶלֶךְ הָעוֹלָם
אֲשֶׁר קִדְּשָׁנוּ בְּמִצְוֹתָיו וְצִוָּנוּ עַל נְטִילַת יָדָיִם.

Baruch   atah   Adonai   Eloheinu   Melech   ha'olam

asher   kid'shanu   bemitzvotav   vetzivanu   al netilat yadayim

Thank you God, Ruler of the world, who makes us holy with mitzvot and tells us to wash our hands.

Sending Messages without Talking

In some families, people wash their hands, say the blessing over washing hands, and then don't speak until everybody is ready to say the blessing over the challah. But if you have something you need to say, you can still send a message without talking! You can even try this on other days of the week.

You can send messages with your face

 I'm happy

 hello

 I want some challah

You can send messages with your body

 I'm fine

 This is taking too long

 I want a hug

You can send messages with your hands

 I love you

 Everything's ok

 I'm doing great!

What message do you want to send to a family member?

Blessing over the Bread

Challah is the delicious braided bread that we eat on Shabbat. Challah is also the last thing we bless before eating our meal. We playfully imagine that the challah might feel upset about being last. So we cover it with a pretty decorated cloth. That way, the challah doesn't see the candles and wine being blessed first. Then we take off the cloth when it's finally time to bless the challah.

Uncover the challah and hold it up so all of the people at the table can see it.

How do you feel when you first see the challah as it appears from beneath its cover?

Say the blessing:

בָּרוּךְ אַתָּה יְיָ אֱלֹהֵינוּ מֶלֶךְ הָעוֹלָם
הַמּוֹצִיא לֶחֶם מִן הָאָרֶץ.

Baruch	atah	Adonai	Eloheinu	Melech	ha'olam

hamotzi
lechem

min
ha'aretz

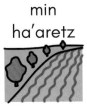

Thank you God, Ruler of the world, who brings bread from the earth.

The challah is cut or torn into pieces.
Take one piece.
Some people put a little salt on their challah before they eat it. This reminds us how people long ago put salt on the food they brought to the Holy Temple in Jerusalem.

Eat the challah.
Challah is a special Shabbat treat. Take time to chew the challah slowly. Notice how the challah tastes, and the way it feels in your mouth.

If you don't want to eat any challah, put it down on your plate.

Shabbat Meal Conversation

After we eat the challah, it's time for our meal to begin! Shabbat dinner is more than just a time to eat. It's a time to talk, maybe sing, and enjoy being together. Here are some questions people might ask each other to start a conversation.

As you talk about your feelings, try to notice how your body and face feel. Do your shoulders droop? Does your belly feel tight inside? Do you smile? Do you feel warm? Or cold? Try to see how other people show their feelings with their bodies and faces too!

 What made you feel happy this week?

 What made you feel upset this week?

 What made you laugh this week?

 What is one way you helped another person this week?

 If you could change one thing about this past week, what would it be?

 What are you looking forward to doing this Shabbat?

 What makes you feel nervous about next week?

 What are you looking forward to doing next week?

Blessing after Our Meal

When the meal is finished, we feel full and content. We pause to thank God for giving us the food we ate. We are grateful every day for the food that keeps us healthy and makes us strong.

Say this blessing:

בָּרוּךְ אַתָּה יְיָ הַזָּן אֶת הַכֹּל.

Baruch	atah	Adonai	hazan	et hakol

Thank you God for giving food to everybody.

What We Do on the Day of Shabbat

Shabbat is a day for each of us to take a break from work and our busy lives. On Shabbat we take time to enjoy the world around us, spend time with the people we love, and think about God.

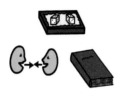

On Shabbat people choose how they want to pause, relax, and recharge. Many families take walks together. Some play card games or board games. Others read books, or perhaps enjoy just sitting around and chatting.

Some families go to synagogue on Shabbat. There we say prayers, hear the Torah read aloud, and spend time with our friends. After synagogue, many families sit down for a tasty Shabbat lunch.

Many people also like to spend some time alone on Shabbat. Perhaps they think back to the past week and look forward to the next. And maybe take a cozy nap in the afternoon.

What activities would you like to do this Shabbat?

Some families are very careful about not doing any work on Shabbat. They might not watch TV, listen to music, write or draw, drive, or go shopping.

Havdalah

Shabbat ends as the sun goes down on Saturday night. We say goodbye to Shabbat and get ready for a new week. This ceremony is called Havdalah, which means "separation." It reminds us that Shabbat is separate from the other days of the week. Even though Shabbat is ending, we know that next Friday night when Shabbat comes again we will be able to pause, restore our energy, and spend time with our family and friends.

Say the blessing:

בָּרוּךְ אַתָּה יְיָ אֱלֹהֵינוּ מֶלֶךְ הָעוֹלָם הַמַּבְדִיל בֵּין קֹדֶשׁ לְחוֹל.

Baruch	atah	Adonai	Eloheinu	Melech	ha'olam

hamavdil bein	kodesh	lechol

Thank you God, Ruler of the world, who separates the holy from the everyday.

What will you do to make the coming week a good one for you and the people around you?

Shavua tov! Have a good week!

Talking to Children about God

Children most easily understand what they can see, hear, and touch, but the notion of God is mysterious and intangible. God is mentioned throughout this book, and your children may be curious and ask questions. Sometimes, our own complicated feelings—perhaps even doubts—make it difficult for us to provide satisfactory answers. However, it is possible to have simple, comfortable conversations with your children about God.

Let children know, through both your words and body language, that it's okay to talk and ask questions about God.

Focus on what our sacred texts say that God *does* as opposed to who God *is*. It is hard for children to understand who God is, especially since God is not visible. The things that our tradition teaches God has done, such as making the world or giving us the Torah, however, are all concrete and visible. They are easier for children to understand.

If your children ask questions to which you don't know the answer, it's okay to say so. You might ask your children what they think or believe, and then share your own thoughts.

Some parents feel uncomfortable explaining traditional Jewish beliefs about God because they don't share those beliefs. Begin your sentences with phrases such as, "The Torah tells us," or "Many Jewish people believe," to convey traditional Jewish views without misrepresenting what you personally believe.